James B. Siders

Songs of a Pleb

James B. Siders

Songs of a Pleb

ISBN/EAN: 9783337181949

Printed in Europe, USA, Canada, Australia, Japan

Cover: Foto ©Thomas Meinert / pixelio.de

More available books at **www.hansebooks.com**

SONGS OF A PLEB,

—BY—

J. W. B. SIDERS, Ph. B., M. L. S.

———

ILLUSTRATED.

POEMS

From the shining flame of knowledge,
  Brothers, you each have a spark,
Fan it with persistent courage,
  It will guide you through the dark.

From each book, each life, or sermon,
  Gather fuel for its flame,
It will light you o'er the river,
  Though it may not give you fame.

Hide it not beneath a bushel,
  Let it all around you shine ;
For in helping hands extended,
  Are the sermons most divine.

Never put aside the talents,
  That the Master gives to you,
Be not like the slothful servant,
  Who was banished from His view.

From the little lake Itasca,
  Bursting forth, a streamlet goes.
Gaining strength from rill and brooklet,
  Till a Mississippi flows.

So, each day, increase your learning,
  Gather from each book so rife,
By and by you'll have a river,
  Reaching to the Sea of Life.

Don't expect to be a hero,
  Only be a *common* man,
Be yourself, and true to nature,
  Copy not another's plan.

O'er the sea a mighty city,
  Built on seven hills, they say,
Mistress of surrounding nations,
  Was not finished in a day.

Stone on stone, then brick and mortar,
  Workmen labored hour by hour,
Growing old in years and dying,
  Ere the city gained its power.

So, my friends, to fame aspiring,
  Don't expect it at a blow;
For the gods who do the grinding,
  Let their mills grind very slow.

MY POEM.

Among the trees where Nature weaves
Fair garlands of the whisp'ring leaves,
I heard my poem as 'twas sung
By ev'ry little flut'ring tongue.

And when I walked the white sea sands,
Where struggling waves reach up their hands,
Perchance in some forgotten lore,
I heard my poem sung, once more.

When in a peasant's cot I lay,
To rest secure till dawn of day,
So deftly, on the thatch, the rain
Rehearsed my poem, there, again.

My poem—ah, how can I tell
Its music or its magic spell
With words so feeble that they seem
To mock my consecrated dream !

PURE IS THE HEART.

Long is the road that hath no ending,
Straight is the path that hath no bending,
Pure is the heart with no pretending,
    That keepeth in the narrow way ;
And few are they, without offending,
    To answer Him on Judgment Day.

Many are the roads, broad, descending,
Many are the mortals onward wending,
Caring not for the wrath impending,
    As often they are led astray.
O, reach thy hands, in truth, befriending
    A brother fallen by the way !

A BLUSH.

"From every blush that kindles in your cheeks,
Ten thousand little loves and graces spring,
To revel in those roses." The heart speaks
Altho' the tongue be still. A little thing
It is ; yet purifies the soul, as rain
Imbrues the air, and feeds the thirsty grain.

The lily may be fair, but then the rose,
With blushing petals set with sparkling dew,
Is best of all—the fairest flower that grows,
The sweetest, most enchanting to the view ;
But 'twould not be so fair, as thus it sips
The dew, had it no blush upon its lips.

Then, school girls, blush ; and in the joyous blush,
Show that you are refined and can perceive,
And you, fair maiden, let the currents rush
To your cheeks, so in faith we may believe
You have a heart ; and lover, like the morn,
As she meets the sun, your pale face adorn.

HIDDEN TREASURES.

There was a bird with russet crest,
   Which sang in the deep, deep wildwood,
In vain I searched for his hidden nest,
   In the bright, bright days of childhood ;
But he always sat in a tree remote,
   To sing his sweetest measure,
And while enchanted by his note,
   I failed to find his treasure.

O, days have come and passed away,
   And the bird has ceased his singing,
But still within my soul to-day,
   I can hear his music ringing;
The lessons then so unforeseen,
   Shall be remembered ever,
Until old Time with sickle keen,
   Life's silver thread shall sever.

For thus I find in after days,
   While seeking worldly pleasures,
We're lured away from duty's ways,
   And miss life's hidden treasures ;
And learn too late in pleasure's train—
   The thoughtless take unheeding—
That our reward's an aching brain,
   A broken heart left bleeding.

THE DEAD PRESIDENT.

The pulse of a Nation now throbs,
   Its music is muffled and low,
Its breath is stifled with sobs,
   Its people are stricken with woe.

And the sable emblem so sad,
   Is seen o'er the threshold at last ;
The flag of our Freedom, once glad,
   Is hanging to-day at half-mast.

Columbia sheddeth a tear
   For the act a demon hath done,
And kneeling beside of the bier,
   She buries a dutiful son.

In a land where liberty dwells,
   Where tyrants were slain long ago,
The heart of the patriot swells
   To witness a hero laid low.

Great God, our dear Father, forgive,
   And pardon the ill-guided man,
For so long as Freedom shall live,
   The hearts of the people ne'er can.

Sept. 26, 1881.

THE SENTINEL.

O'er the sea in a distant land,
Where rivers wash the golden sand,
In forests deep, recluse and wild,
Where elands feed, so meek and mild,
Where wild beasts come to feed at will,
Beside the lake so clear and still,
There is a bird with watchful eye,
Which utters oft its warning cry.

When its companion lies asleep,
And Zulu-men unto him creep,
Or when he wends his unknown way
Through jungles dense at close of day,
The crouching lions from the lair
Await to spring ere he's aware ;
But lest they take him by surprise,
The bird forewarns him with its cries.

Vice is the savage with his spear,
Whose stealthy steps thou canst not hear,
Or crouching lion in his lair,
That seeks thy ruin everywhere;
Thy conscience is the bird, my friend,
Which doth upon thy soul attend,
O, heed its voice, awake and flee,
Ere hidden foe o'ercometh thee !

DECORATION DAY.

This morn, a glory-giving sun
   Smiled on a peaceful land,
I heard the booming of a gun,
   The music of a band ;
I saw the flow'rs, the grand display,
And knew 'twas decoration day.

The children came with eager hands,
   The maidens in their bloom,
And to the music of the bands,
   They sought each soldier's tomb —
Such heroes in a land like ours,
Should have, at least, its rarest flow'rs.

They sleep ; and many watchful stars
   Look down on them to-night,
Recounting all their wounds and scars,
   And deaths, defending Right ;
And while our star-set banner waves,
Shall we forget their humble graves ?

SEMPER IDEM.

The same strange birds in the wildwoods sing,
The same sweet blooms come with ev'ry spring,
The same green vines to their towers cling—
   The same, yet ever, ever new.

The same old trees in the forest grow,
The same old streams to the ocean flow,
The same old peaks lift their caps of snow—
  The same, yet ever, ever new.

The same old stars, resplendent, shine above,
The same old spheres in their orbits move,
The same sweet tale is ever told with love—
  The same, yet ever, ever new.

AKIN.

The river flowing to the sea,
With gentle shimmer as it glides,
Could not exist, but cease to be,
Were there no rills to swell its sides.

The tranquil lake, to nature true,
  Reflecting back her tender glow,
Would soon exhale its waters blue,
  Were there no hidden springs below.

And so would ev'ry human heart,
  That keeps the world, at large, akin,
Be thus deserted and apart,
  Were there no springs of love within.

IN VAIN.

There is no fragrant flower that blows,
  On shady brink or fertile plain,
That hides its head so no màn knows
The rifted rock whereon it grows,
Or where 'tis hid, as on he goes;
  But what must bloom and die in vain.

There is no song of warbling bird,
  No gentle note, no mellow strain,
No oft repeated, trusting word,
(A sign of hope, true or absurd,)
Lest it by eager ears be heard;
  But what is sung or said in vain.

There is no star that shines at night,
  Unseen, unknown in His domain,
So far away that in its might
It fails to send to us its light,
Altho' it be intensely bright;
  But what must shine and shine in vain.

There is no throbbing, pulsing heart,
  That beats a march in life's dull train,
That has not felt the thrilling smart
From Cupid's shy, unerring dart,
Which he to mortal can impart;
  But what has throbbed and beat in vain.

WHEN I AM DEAD.

When I am dead,
Come thou not near the humble grave,
Where sleeps this head ;
But let me have the rest I crave.

For no one knows
The mysteries beyond the vale,
Where mortal goes
To take his place with spirits pale.

Come thou not near,
To sigh, or moan, or idly weep,
Lest I should hear,
And startle from my peaceful sleep.

Let willows tall,
And cedars green, the year around,
Sing madrigal
With softest breeze and gentlest sound.

Let slender vine,
And plant that loves the silent shade,
Their leaves entwine,
To hide the mound where I am laid.

For all this life,
Forever seems to be oppressed
With cares and strife,
And in the grave I may have rest.

Come thou not nigh;
But pass me by with gentlest tread,
And do not sigh,
Or scoff to wake the restful dead.

WEIRDNESS.

O, blow, ye bleak winds, blow,
Send forth thy drifting snow,
And hide me from my woe.

Blow thou thy cutting blast,
And while it moans apast,
I may find rest at last.

O, hum thy god-lent strain
On sash and window-pane,
And soothe my aching brain.

For I am faint from strife,
From bustling toils of life,
From cares and troubles rife.

O, night-wind, sing a tune,
O, clouds, shut out the moon,
Then rest may follow soon.

Then I shall sleep away
The cares I had to-day,
Ere dawns the morning gray.

NATURE'S MELODIES.

When rosy morn had tinged the skies,
  And forth I strolled for exercise ;
From ev'rything seemed to arise
  All nature in her melodies.

I sat beneath a forest tree,
  Where birdlings hopped about in glee,
And through its boughs, most gloriously,
  The winds sang nature's melody.

I stood where crystal waters poured,
  I saw the cataract which roared,
And in the water's noisy spree,
  Was nature's deepest melody.

I saw the vivid lightning flash,
  I stopped, and heard the awful crash,
But in that crash so sharp and free,
  Was nature's loudest melody.

'Twas night, weary, I lay abed,
  Storm-clouds, so dark, o'erhung my head ;
Upon the roof the raindrops played
  Fond nature's sweetest serenade.

THE MOUND BUILDERS.

Far back in the flight of fleeting ages,
When the infant Earth wore her first garments,
Methinks the Creator let live and thrive—
Ere the building of the fair Parthenon,
Ere the Coliseum was archetyped—
A race unknown to us, save by their works.
We behold the ruins of their cities—
Cities built by sensible architects;
But now buried deep away by the hand
Of iron-hearted Time, who levels all;
And our hearts are awed within us, and we
Recoil in mute amazement from the scene.

Were they a people warlike in pursuits,
Savage and sanguine, and the earthy mounds
Rude places of defense?   Or shall we think
Them rather to be as the Pyramids,
Vaults in which to inter the departed?
None is left to answer save the winds
That kiss the face of Ocean and return
To play among the flowers and then repose
In the deep valleys—cradles of the storm :
"They are concealed, still their works outlive them,
Their citadels and their strange temples stood,
And the swain broke the glebe with the droll ox,
Which time hath chang'c to a shaggy bison,
And turned him loose upon the field to feed.

Anon, silken dresses rustled in the streets,
And then fortune's contending jewels shone,
Then envious eyes encountered, and all
Was explained away for the time at hand.
Then lovers walked and wooed, and pulsing hearts
Beat a high tenor to the winning words
Of a curious language, long forgot,
And when the blush of silent evening came,
The sounding lute won each one from his care,
And when the hall in splendor shone, each one
Came in attire of fashions unrevealed,
And danced to mystic music in delight.

So the world grew evil as it grew old,
Till the elements warred with elements,
And their contentions destroyed the living.
Then time heaped clay upon their mould'ring forms,
And decked their forsaken fields with a sward,
And set green trees along the rivers."
Thus the wind sang of the long departed,
While along the streets busy crowds rushed forth,
That had no thought for eternity gone ;
And said to me : " Some idler of the future
May sit and think your relics o'er and o'er,
As you to-day have mused on those of yore. "

SOME EYES.

"They are the books, the arts, the academies,
That show, contain and nourish all the world."
——Shakespeare.

The eyes—"the windows of the soul!"
That view the world in all her pride ;
Some love, some hate and some console,
Some laugh, some cry and some deride.

Some ask, assert and some entreat,
Some penetrate you, some command,
Some prowl you o'er from head to feet,
Some flash and shock you as you stand.

Some gentle, some calm, some sedate,
Some mirthful, shining bright with glee ;
Each has a story to relate—
A meaning which we all may see.

The fair *blue* eye which seems to take
Its gentle color from the sky,
Will learn and love and keep awake
With ready question and reply.

The eyes which are so *large* and *bright*,
Show thoughtful minds and tastes refined,
And *gray-eyed* girls with soul and might,
Will prove to you most true and kind.

Imaginative, false, untrue,
The eyes most jealous and malign,
Are eyes of *green* or vacant hue,
The eyes that see the least divine.

The *dark* eye shows the gift of power,
The *black* eye—oh, beware, I pray !
So fickle, changeful as the hour,
Loves first, then hates within a day.

Most faithful, though, of all in all,
Are *hazel* eyes, so tame and good,
Eyes to obey at ev'ry call,
Eyes to esteem you if they would.

O, eyes ! Oh, "windows of the soul !"
Let in the light from heaven's blue,
That we may see from pole to pole,
" The Good, the Beautiful, the True."

THE SEASONS.

O, BREEZES OF THE SOUTH.

O, breezes of the south, where orange blossoms grow,
O, breezes of the south, where winters never snow,
O, breezes of the south, for thee I'll ever sing,
O, breezes of the south, sweet harbingers of spring !

O, breezes of the south, come touch me with thy wings,
Come laden, bringing sweets from lands of Aztec kings,
Come with thy singing birds and dancing butterflies,
Come with thy freighted breath from summer tinted skies !

O, breezes of the south, drive Boreas from his throne,
O, melt his icy heart, though be it hard as stone,
O, breezes, drive him hence and let him dwell alone,
Among the glist'ning icebergs in the Frigid zone.

SPRING. (In April.)

Here a shadow, there a beam ;
　　Here a cloudlet, there a shower ;
Here a brooklet, there a stream ;
　　Here a leaflet, there a flower.

Here a twitter, there a song,
　　Here a caw, and there a chatter ;
Then a silence of the throng ;
　　Here again's the pitter-patter !

Plow-boy, taken by surprise,
　　Seeks a temporary shelter ;
School girl, as she homeward hies,
　　Feels the drops begin to pelt her.

　　*　　*　　*　　*　　*　　*　　*

Lo ! the clouds are all aglow,
   And the birds again are flying ;
And there is a second bow,
   Just above the one that's dying.

April, fourth child of the year,
   Nothing art thou ever staid in ;
First a smile and then a tear ;
   Thou art like a pouting maiden !

IN MAY.

Now is the Spring,
When thrushes sing,
And ev'ry thing
Seems to wear a smile,
The flowers bloom,
The swallows come
To make a home
With us here awhile.

The humming bees
Among the trees,
In tranquil breeze
Sip their nectars sweet,
And butterflies
Fair as the skies
Betimes surprise
The flow'rs at our feet.

With anxious looks,
The boys with hooks,
Along the brooks
Ramble all the day ;
In dreamy whirls,
The laughing girls
Bedeck their curls
In a sweet display.

Along the way
Where lovers stray
The flow'rs so gay
Fold their gentle wings ;
For ev'ry day
In merry May
They'll hear them say
Many artful things.

O merry Spring,
Spread out thy wing
O'er ev'ry thing,
Let Nature rejoice ;
To Flora bring
Thy offering,
And let us sing
In triumphant voice.

SUMMER. (In July.)

I hear the busy reaper's song,
  An ever welcome strain ;
As thus it sings it all day long,
  Down in the golden grain ;
And as I listen to the chime,
I know it tells of summertime.

I hear the merry voices speak,
  I heard in days of yore ;
When children play'd at " hide and seek "
  About the threshing floor ;
As o'er the new mown hay they'd climb,
In those sweet days of summertime.

Beneath the stately elm tree's shade,
  When winds and skies were fine,
Upon the bark with clumsy blade,
  I carved her name and mine ;
But they've been changed by storm and rime,
Since that fair day in summertime.

When up some stream in search of bass,
  I hear the heron's cry,
And from the tangled brakes of grass,
  I see the wood-ducks fly ;
I think, ah me, oft in my prime,
Have I thus strolled in summertime.

And from the bridge, near by the mill,
   I watch the fishes glide,
And see, betimes when winds are still,
   The glimmer of a side,
And act my part in pantomime,
With those who love the summertime.

At eve, the tinkle of the fold,
   The lowing of the kine,
Repeat the same old story told
   Unto this heart of mine ;
While bubbling brooklet tells in rhyme
About the dreamy summertime.

The same old stars shine in the sky,
   The silent moon looks on,
I hear the wood-bird's plaintive cry ;
   The cricket's song, anon ;
And think that life, although sublime,
Is but a fleeting summertime.

AUTUMN. (Song of Boreas.*)

My bands are playing in the pines,
I am advancing with my lines ;
You can hear my chariot wheels,
When e'er the sylvan forest reels ;
The river hears me, and stands still,
His quiv'ring heart with spears I fill,
And thus before me all must fly,
Ha, ha! a king, a king reign I !

The birds, the flow'rs, and all of these,
Which are friends of Hesperian breeze,
Or which love the Zephrian lay,
I either kill or drive away ;
My banners through the sky I fling,
As my dead foes lie withering ;
My voice is heard both low and high,
Ho, ho ! a king, a king reign I !

I come, I come ; the many feet
Of my steeds are the snow and sleet ;
My captains are the icebergs tall,
The frozen sea, my strongest wall ;
My helmets, shields and spears of ice
Are made with many a sly device :
You cannot stay me should you try ;
Behold, a king, a king reign I.

*The North Wind, believed to have been kept in a cave, and loosed at a certain
bidding. Some say Boreas was ruler of the north wind and kept it in a bag.

                                                          MYTH.

And with my warriors, tried and brave,
Who lived within my hidden cave,
Now, o'er the world I take my way,
Chilling and killing night and day ;
Ycur woolen shields and coats of fur,
Will not my ravages deter ;
My ear is deaf to ev'ry cry,
For now, a king, a king reign I.

WINTER.   (January.)

Bold January,
Month, cold and dreary,
The Year's first child,
So fierce and wild !

How shall we greet you,
Or, as friends, meet you,
And thus beguile the time,
In this our arctic clime ?

" Oh men of learning,
With your hearts yearning,—
Great men of all classes,
Gay lads and fair lasses,
I'll tell you all in rhyme,
How you can pass the time :

" Oh, I am cheerily,
Yes, and so merrily
Made with rare books,
And pleasant looks,
And fast sleigh-riding,
Skating and sliding,
Hunting and gaming,
Catching and taming,
Wooing and whiling,
Winning and smiling,
Funning and laughing,
Chatting and chaffing,
Learning and knowing,
Coming and going,
Cheering and choosing,
Sitting and musing
Around our fires burning,
As the world goes turning.

" Still my cold breath
Hath chilled to death
The leaves of flowers,
And summer bowers ;
So branches once stirr'd
By breeze and wild bird,
Ache with grim pain
For summer again.

" But you'll gladly endure
My rough weather, I'm sure,
For my many treasures,
Little joys and pleasures,
And be glad to see me here,
As the first child of the Year."

FONS JUVENTIS.

Ho, westward, westward, westward!
   The sails are courting the wind ;
A ship leaves on the billows,
   A river of foam behind.

And smaller grows old Spain-land,
   A speck within the blue,
Till in the dim horizon,
   It fades and sinks from view.

The strange sea-birds come flying,
   And light upon the ship ;
I fancy they are smiling
   At such a novel trip.

The calm, old moon is shining,
   And often takes a peep,
Then hides behind a cloudlet,
   That's floating o'er the deep.

The zephyrs thro' the rigging,
   Sigh many a mocking tune ;
While o'er the silver waters,
   The ship glides with the moon.

Sometimes a frighted mermaid
  Looks up from 'neath the wave,
And shakes her silken tresses,
  Then hurries to her cave.

But who's the happy sailor,
  Who's heart o'erflows with glee,
At visions of his childhood,
  And fountain pure and free?

'Tis Juan Ponce de Leon,
  A daring man from Spain,
In search of " Fons Juventis,"
  Embarking on the main.

He calls his men around him,
  And asks them all to dine,
And listen to this story,
  And taste his Spanish wine :

" There is an isle, Bimini,
  Where mortals ne'er grow old,
Who drink the magic waters
  From goblets made of gold.

I know 'tis only nature
  For man to cling to life ;
But now no longer anxious,
  We'll rest secure from strife.

For now our ship is gliding,
  And ere yon moon shall wane,
Beyond the gray Tortugas,
  We'll take new lives again.

And then we'll smile defiance
  At Death, the spectral ghost,
And tell old Time, the father,
  We spurn his dying host.

And where we've had misfortunes,
  We'll profit by the past,
And live a life most perfect
  With those we've loved at last.

For man ne'er sees his errors,
  His wrecks, his griefs, his scars ;
Or how he's sailed life's ocean,
  And hung upon its bars ;

Till half his time allotted,
  His three score years and ten,
Are written in that record :
  ' The Destiny of Men.' "

       *   *   *   *   *   *   *

So spake the gallant hero,
  And drank his Spanish wine,
And praised the living fountain,
  Where crystal waters shine.

Then onward with his sailors,
    He sped for many a mile,
His eye upon th' horizon,
    His heart upon the isle.

Thus came he to a country,
    On *Pascua Florida*,
Refreshed by many a river,
    Beset with many a bay.

He anchored in its harbors,
    And claimed it for his king,
And searched thro' many a forest,
    And drank from many a spring ;

But never found Bimini,
    For which he searched so long,
Or life-renewing fountain,
    So heralded in song.

He, thwarted in his efforts,
    Died of a mortal wound
Made by a savage hunter
    To save his hunting ground.

But there will be no dying
    To such a hero's fame,
Forever and forever
    Will echo back his name.

And Spaniards will remember,
 And look with love and pride
Toward the Western Country,
 Where such a hero died.

For from its vernal beauty,
 Sweet buds and fragrant flow'rs,
He named it ere departing;
 "Florida—land of flowers."

LOVE SONGS.

O, MAIDEN FAIR.

Air.—" The Bohemian Girl."

O, maiden fair, turn not away
   Thy pure and tender eye,
Forget the past and love again,
   Or, weeping, I shall die ;
No other soul, no other heart
   Shall ever hear my tale ;
O, drive me not by word or act,
   Where wounded spirits wail.

I could not live one day and see
   Another claim thy hand,
I could not die and keep my soul
   Content in Spirit-land,
And know that we, undone by fate,
   Must ever stay apart,
Or think that he who loves thee less,
   Had won thy maiden heart.

O, maiden fair, trust not the tale,
   Which other lips may tell,
Believe in none except the heart,
   That feels and loves so well !
How canst thou treat with careless grace,
   My love, my look, my sigh ?
O, speak to me, and love again,
   Or, weeping, I shall die !

THOU ART NOTHING TO ME NOW.

Thou art nothing to me now ;
  Cold as the Alpine snows,
  Cold as the blast that blows,
  Cold as the words which froze
  This heart, am I to those
Who are nothing to me now.

Thou art nothing to me now ;
  Those lips so fondly pressed,
  Those eyes with smiles caressed,
  Those hands in jewels dressed,
  The love one day professed—
All, are nothing to me now.

Thou art nothing to me now ;
  Farewell, we meet no more,
  I leave my native shore
  To search the wide world o'er
  For hearts, true to the core—
Thou art nothing to me now.

ONLY A DREAM.

I had a dream of mystic lore,
  Which seems to haunt me as I rove ;
I shall forget it nevermore—
  I dreamed that I kissed my love.

The sun had hid his blazing glare,
  Night wept dew drops from above,
And in my visions, all so fair,
  I dreamed that I kissed my love.

I tho't that we were strolling nigh
  The cot within the shady grove,
And when I turned to say 'good bye,'
  I dreamed that I kissed my love.

I tho't I took her hand in mine,
  That little hand without a glove,
And when she did her cheek incline—
  I dreamed that I kissed my love.

Within'that last look at the gate,
  I thought a trembling passion strove,
But thus it was decreed by fate.—
  I dreamed that I kissed my love.

O, I care not for silly jokes ;
  But then I was to madness drove,
When I found 'twas all a hoax,
  And *dreaming that I kissed my love.*

WHEN I DREAM.

When I dream,
  There stands a spirit near my bed,
    And it doth seem
  To speak of days forever fled—
When I dream.

When I dream,
There comes my friend that used to play
Along life's stream,
In all her youthful, sweet array—
When I dream.

When I dream,
That maiden face I used to hold
In high esteem,
Bends o'er my pillow as of old —
When I dream.

When I dream,
Those eyes look down and seem to say,
As thus they beam,
The words I heard in boyhood's day —
When I dream.

When I dream,
Those lips appear to touch my brow,
As to redeem
A long lost pledge or broken vow—
When I dream.

When I dream,
My heart once more begins to quake
With hopeful gleam
That long was dead—then I awake
From my dream.

CLARIBEL.

Chorus :

Fare you well, Claribel,
  I am weeping, Claribel,
And my grief I cannot tell—
  Fare you well, fare you well.

In the happy, golden past,
  Not a cloud my life o'ercast ;
But they've come to me at last,
  Like a tempest's howling blast.

O, your heart is like a stone
  In a desert place, alone,
And I've made of it a throne,
  Where I worshiped with my own.

Give me back, again, my heart,
  Heal the wound from Cupid's dart,
For I feel its cruel smart—
  Loose your toils and I'll depart.

Let some true heart for me glow,
  One that is not cold as snow,
By its wooing I may know
  It hath love and can bestow.

I LOVE THE SEA.

I love the sea with his great, gray rocks ;
I love the sea with his hoary locks ;
But why do I love the great, deep sea,
When he taketh my true-love from me ?

I love the sea with his happy isles ;
I love the sea when his great face smiles ;
I love the sea --- oh, how can it be,
When he taketh my true-love from me ?

I love the sea with his hidden gold,
With his gems of purest light, untold ;
But why do I love with heart so free,
When he taketh my true-love from me ?

I love the sea as he clasps his hands,
Or holds them out to stroke the sands —
O, joy must fill his great heart with glee,
As he taketh my true-love from me !

I love the sea, and his ships as well,
And their finny sails which rise and swell ;
For once, as I watched the golden sea,
He brought my true-love back to me.

A PURITAN MAID'S SONG.

We stroll'd upon the yellow sands,
He clasped me with his trembling hands ;
He sailed away to foreign lands,
    Across the deep, blue sea.

He wrote to me he would be true,
Although his face I could not view,
And, in a year, he would renew
    His vow of love for me.

The summer flowers came back again,
He sailed upon the doubtful main —
Alas! alas! my heart's deep pain,
    His ship was lost at sea.

His grave was made among the pearls,
Where mermaid with her silken curls,
His direful story now unfurls
    In her strange minstrelsy.

And in my dreams of angel bands,
I see him as he waiting stands,
Still holding out his snowy hands
    To keep his vow with me.

DEAR HEART, YOU SAY YOU LOVE ME.

Dear heart, you say you love me,
 Your speech I scarce believe,
They say that words are fickle,
 And *words* sometimes deceive.

Dear heart, you say you love me,
 You greet me with a smile ;
But *smiles* are seldom earnest,
 So often they beguile.

Dear heart, you say you love me,
 You seek to win by stealth,
Your *presents* do not move me,
 Love is not sold for wealth.

Dear heart, you say you love me,
 When you only love my *gold*,
O, *love* can never issue
 From looks and gifts so cold.

Dear heart, you say you love me,
 A tear falls on my breast,
A clasp of hands in silence,
 Is more than all the rest.

O, LOVE!

O, love, dear love,
They tell me that thy beauty will decay,
And love, sweet love,
Thy graceful charms, too soon, will pass away.

But love, true love,
Thy heart will ever be the same to me,
And love, my love,
Thy soul contain its tender purity.

Then love, sweet love,
Old Time shall never drive Good Cheer away ;
For love, old love,
He can but take from us this house of clay.

O, FRIGID LOOKS!

O, frigid looks, averted eyes!
Here, take the gifts I used to prize ;
The frost of negligence severe,
Has slain the flow'rs I held so dear.

I would not be a clog — a weight
To hinder e'en the one I hate !
O, take the urn which holds the dust
Of plighted love, once sacred trust !

Had I a friend, had she a heart
That could be won by sundry art,
By jewels rare, or bags of gold,
I'd know her by its love so cold.

I could not sleep, I could not rest
With dreams of such gifts on my breast ;
O, take them back, return my own,
The cage is naught with songster flown !

ESTRANGED.

Thy smiles, thy sighs, thy tears
    Have ceased so long ago ;
The flowers of early years
    Have perished in the snow.

The luster of thine eyes,
    The grasp of eager hands—
Affection's strongest ties,
    Are now but broken bands.

Thy hesitating step,
    The melancholy glance
From eyes that often wept
    Within thy lonely manse ;

Are evidence to me
 Sufficiently to prove
That all was coquetry,
 And had no touch of love.

Thy sighs, thy smiles, thy tears
 Were counterfeit and base,
Within thy looks and fears
 I can discern the trace.

O, give me of that love,
 Replete and free from gall,
Kept consecrate by Jove,
 Or give me none at all.

BANISHED.

Alas, alas, we've said farewell;
 No plight or troth remains,
No charm to break the phantom spell
 That keeps the heart in chains.

That dreamy eye, that rosy cheek,
 That face with ready smile,
That tongue which did my praises speak,
 Would now with scorn revile.

Those lips in love that once were press'd,
  Now at my coming pale,
And fain would offer a protest ;
  But then they somehow fail.

Oh, why for pride's ostensive sake,
  Wilt thou offend thy love,
And cause two hearts in grief to break,
  That faithful yet might prove ?

Oh, God, forgive the erring heart
  That scorns to be humane,
And heal, oh heal, with wondrous art,
  The one which loves in vain !

SOME DAY.

Some day, as thro' this life I press,
While battling Fate or fleeing Time,
I may behold in tenderness,
A face I loved in manhood's prime.

Some day, along the busy street,
Thro' mazes of the dim Unknown,
Perchance, some angel I may meet,
Will tell me something of my own.

Some day, while struggling in the race,
Which leads to Fame's uncertain goal,
Perhaps I'll meet her face to face,
O, then, what joy shall fill my soul !

Some day, my heart shall eat its fill
From Fortune's board of bread and wine,
And all my anxious fears be still ;
When I am hers and she is mine.

FRANGIPANI.

I watch the dying embers play
   Upon the hearth to-night ;
They shine like twinkling stars, away
   In untold realms of light.

And as I watch them as they glow
   And kindle into flame,
I think of one who long ago
   Glowed in this heart the same.

The German and the ball were o'er,
   And I, an ardent guest,
Obeying her, that night I wore
   A rose upon my breast.

Her eyes displayed a lustrous light
  Which seemed to know my doom,
As in her jeweled hand, so white,
  She held a sweet perfume.

For I was smitten with her pun,
  Her wit, her repartee ;
Before her beauty's queenly throne,
  I bent the willing knee.

And when I asked her if she'd wed
  Her heart and hand to mine ;
She only bowed her knowing head,
  And seemed the more divine.

I whisper'd low, that with a word,
  My future she could bless ;
She said ; " In me 'twould be absurd,
  Then, not to answer, yes ! "

Somehow, her vase of sweet perfume
  Was spilled upon my breast —
By accident we may presume —
  But you can guess the rest.

Old Time hath pass'd on wings so fleet,
  Still he cannot consume
A recollection that is sweet,
  And pleasing as perfume.

The night-wind prowls about the door,
   And shakes the pane with cold ;
I hear a rustle as of yore,
   Within each curtain's fold ;

And think 'tis but a silken dress,
   With all its sweet perfume,
As oft it moved with gentleness
   About the hallowed room.

The rose is dead—its beauty fled,
   And she is in the tomb,
And oft instead of roses red,
   I smell the sweet perfume.

For Time hath cleft a heart and left
   It ling'ring here in gloom —
A thing of weft, a thing bereft
   Of all but sweet perfume.

So, I'll retire as doth my fire,
   Which ceaseth to illume,
And to inspire the living lyre
   With thoughts of sweet perfume.

O, TELL ME, WHAT IS LOVE !

O, tell me not the sun is flame,
   The moon reflected light,
Or how the constant stars became
   The watches of the night ;

That night's the mother of the day,
   The morning of the noon,
Or beauty's charms will soon decay,
   And youth depart too soon ;

That pleasure's but a ready snare,
   Its best reward a sigh,
And oft before we can prepare,
   Our time has come to die.

O, tell me not, I know too well
   These lessons, and approve,
But tell, O Fates—Minerva tell,
   O, tell me what is love ?

FIRST LOVE.

Thou art my little love, thou art
Queen of my soul and joy of heart ;
Before thy throne, my smiles, my tears,
I'll sacrifice for many years.

Had I a scroll on which to write,
Large as yon sky so clear and bright,
And were my ink the deep, blue sea,
Ne'er could I tell my love for thee.

Should Orpheus come and tune his lute,
Whose music could, beyond dispute,
Ensnare the fierce le-vi-a-than,
'Twould not move me as thy love can.

As sparkling dew, at midnight hour,
So falleth on a thirsty flow'r,
And to its leaves new life imparts,
So cometh love unto our hearts.

A SERENADE.

Last night, I dreamed of you, I dreamed of you ;
Your angel face came to my view, came to my view,
With songs of the beautiful, songs of the good and true.

CHORUS.

O, Mari! Time, time is ever ;
Meet me by the cool, mossy stream ;
O, Mari ! Leave, leave me never,
Love is like a sweet, tranquil dream.

Down where the shy, little dove, little dove,
Look'd forth from its hidden nest above, nest above,
It sang to its happy mate, as first I told my love.

CHORUS.

But time now has chang'd the place, chang'd the place,
Has chang'd my heart, has chang'd your face, has chang'd your face,
Still there is left for me, love, hope and queenly grace.
CHORUS.

Life's dream will soon be o'er, will soon be o'er,
Love's happy songs I'll sing no more, I'll sing no more ;
None then will ever know what our hearts shall keep in store.

MY LITTLE MARIANNE.

In the little town of Eaton,
    Near by a bubbling stream,
Where the poets love to wander,
    And music seems to dream,
Liv'd a little rosy maiden,
    Her name was Marianne,
I learned to love her dearly,
    Long before I was a man.
        CHORUS.

        Then come, ye bards, and tune your harps,
            To sing of one so fair ;
        For all my love for Marianne,
            Was " castles in the air."

Now speak your thoughts, say what you will,
    Of lovers true and blest ;
But of them all on this great earth,
    A poet-love is best ;
But by and by some other lad,
    To love her, soon began,
And ere I knew, he won away
    My little Marianne.

So I, the broken hearted youth,
  (For thus the story ran,)
Was left to sing my awful fate,
  And wail for Marianne.
Thus end our little love scenes,
  With little lovers fair,
Like fleeting dreams of Fairy Land,
  And " castles in the air."

SWEET ANNIE.

The farmer plows, the farmer sows,
The farmer reaps, the farmer mows ;
But I care not how all that goes,
When I think of thee, sweet Annie.
The winds may blow, the waves roll high,
On life's deep sea, for aught care I ;
But I cannot restrain a sigh,
When I think of thee, sweet Annie.

The mock-bird sits upon a stake,
And sings his song, my heart to break ;
But he can only make it quake
For a kiss from thee, sweet Annie;
And hidden in the tree above,
So sweetly, sings the turtle-dove,
Just to remind me of the love
That I have for thee, sweet Annie.

The gentle wind sings thro' the trees,
The soft waves roll the deep, blue seas,
These are nature's charms to please
Winsome hearts like thine, sweet Annie.
Ev'ry science and ev'ry art
Might from this universe depart,
Should'st thou remain to charm my heart,
With thy love, my bonnie Annie.

TO A MEMBER OF THE CLUB.

Farewell, sweet girl, farewell,
No longer wouldst thou stay,
Yet the western zephyrs tell
Of foot-falls far away.

To me no cupid's dart,
Could pierce a soul so well,
But thou art gone, dear heart!
Farewell, sweet girl, farewell.

ERRATA.

Page 112, line 11 from first, read *Or*, for "Our."

Page 115, line 11 from first, read, *shun* for "show."

Page 117, in the note, read *infinitesimal*.

Page 119, line 2, in second piece, read *say* for "play."

Page 121, after "two," period for comma.

Page 121, line 4 has too much "*sugar*" in it.,

HUMOROUS MISCELLANY.

"TOO TOO."

The Vassar girls are still ahead—
  Not in the wax they chew,
In that *per se*, I've heard it said
  They seem to be "too too;"

But with the thoughts they have in mind,
  Which they present to you
By cunning synonyms, "refined."
  Which always are "too too."

Last month, a prince of regal state,
  As rich as any Jew,
Proposed to wed a graduate;
  She said he was "too too."

Thus of his wealth across the sea,
  A picture fair he drew,
Concluding with his colony :
  (Which she pronounced "too too.")

Harry:—"In Afric's bright and sunny land,
  I have broad fields so green;
Wilt thou accept my proffered hand,
  And be the ruling queen?"

Sierra:—" Sahara, do not give me Air,
    So close to Timbuctu,
    Your proposition is quite fair ;
    But then it is too too. "

Harry:—" Sweet maiden, pray what meanest thou
    By those two words so chaste ?
    Come hither and I'll show thee how
    The men survey'd the *waste.* "

Sierra:—" Sir, I'm astonished at your taste !
    When others are in view,
    He that surveys a lady's *waist,*
    Is utterly too too !

I Caffir no young Fellah's hand,
    Your way, sir, now pursue ;
    Your bold request I cannot stand ;
    Because it is too too !

Poughkeepsie a bulldog in his shed,
    That lies in wait for you,
    And could you learn what's in *his* head,
    You'd think *he* was too too !

What ! have you Senegal, good sir,
    But who would thus eschew
    An offer so averse to her
    From one who is too too ? "

Harry:—" O a sis thou must be an Air,
    Perplexing, too, I own ;
    But do not drive me to despair,
    I offer thee a throne. "

Sierra:—" Say, Harry it would make me Tsad
    To cross the waters blue,
    And then poor mother would go mad
    To think I was too too."

Harry:—" Sierra Le one hand in this,
    Fear not thy mother's wrath ;
    She'd have to Guard,-if-u-I miss,
    The dangers of thy path ! "

Sierra:—" I've no Good Hope, Suez you please,
    My answer's firm and true ;
    I'll live an Airless maid of ease
    Before I'll wed too too.

    So go to Guinea with your wealth,
    I hold no man in lieu ;
    I think the climate for my health
    Too utterly too too."

Harry:—" The Region of eternal Gum
    Is far across the sea,
    The place so often sought by some
    Young ladies fair, like thee. "

Sierra:—" The Bight of Benin, too, is there ;
    A bite that none can chew,
    I'd be so vext that I could swear,
    To get a bite too too ! "

So then, the good prince bow'd his head,
    And sobbed a sad " boo-hoo ; "
    Because the girl he could not wed
    Had said he was " too too."

Harry:—" Alas, this parting gives me pain,
    Dear heart, but then adieu,
    I'll sail across the surging main,
    Because thou art 'too too!' "

THE NAU(GH)TICAL LOVERS.

O, listen friend, while I unfurl
    A sailor's little sail,
And for its truth I reefer you
    To steamer, " U. S. Mail."

Jack C. Foam was a sailor buoy,
    And rowed upon the waves,
He had seen thousands bite the dust,
    And sink to watery graves.

He always let his iron flukes
    Drag near the eastern coast ;
For here was moored a little maid,
    Who shorely loved him most.

He often mist'er while at sea,
    Which rigg'd him full and sore,
And made him wish hi sea sy life
    Upon the brine was oar.

He said ; "'F I don't s-s-top mizzen her,
   I'll be a jolly b-b(l)oat,"
So he again began to pour,
   And to his gal'e wrote :

" Dear h'art, I am to duty tide,
   Fo river by the main,
Reel ease me with a single word,
   And calm this surging brain.

Can oe consult me at the wall,
   Near by your father's lot ?
Y'acht to meet me if you luff me,
   Although he bids you knot.

I know you're not a nau(gh)tical,
   But then you are my stay,
I will not give you wind, lass, dear,
   So meet me there, I (s)pray,"

Her father rudder little note,
   And loudly he did rower,
And said he'd spanker if he did
   Ketch her with Jack once more.

So he began to harp(o)on John,
   And harp on Nanna dear,
And cut her with hi sword so keen —
   She shed a salty tear.

He said he'd larboard long enough
  As tiller of the " sile,"
And he would s(ch)ooner die than see
  A tar-tar spend his pile.

Miss Nanna reeled and coalered up,
  And bit her lips and vowed
That she Jack's figurehead would be,
  As o'er the main he plowed.

Days came, days went, the waves roll'd high,
  No seaman came in sight,
She thought his brig-a-dear device,
  And Jack a water sprite.

One morning Towser gave a barque,
  She to the lattice flew,
And there upon the wall sat Jack,
  To hold an interview.

The father stern with his commands,
  Bid Jack to cut away,
Or he would be to him a wheel
  To churn him into spray.

The flying Nan' with pennant hair,
  Across the yard then ran,
And fell a-weeping on a log,
  Near by her sailor man.

"O, Johnny dear, you warship me,
　　I cannot tell y'awl ;
I see we air in deep distress,
　　Don't let you r anchor fall."

Jack saw the error of his weigh,
　　And caught her in the squall ;
He could not tarry long, but tho't
　　He'd skipper o'er the wall.

He had a nocean on his mind,
　　A grating at the heart,
To sail away with her just then
　　To some bah Nanna mart.

"Now, who can pinnace to this spot,
　　I'd like to know?" said Jack,
"For I am fleet of foot, and you
　　Shall tell me how to tack."

He tho't he'd lugger to his boat,
　　And steer 'er for the ship,
But then, alas for J. & N.
　　They never made the trip.

For down beneath the surging waves,
　　Unseen by mortal eye,
A devil fish was singing there
　　His "swi et by and by."

So up he came unto the top,
　　And snugly tuck'd them in,
And pressed them to his heavin' chest
　　Within his little fin.

But Jack hung to his diving belle,
　　So all the fishes said,
Until their mangled skel-e-tons
　　Were mingled with the dead.

MORAL.

Now all ye pa-ri-ents on the coast,
　　I pray you keep good heart,
For thus the cunning devil-fish
　　Has vowed to take your part ;

And if your daughters run away
　　To marry sailor men,
He'll catch them every one for you,
　　And take them to his den.

PRESSED FLOWERS.

Ah, she was fair!
And I remember, too, the very night,
'Twas when I graduated.   Dressed in white,
I saw her there.

When I essayed,
And bands, with music sweet, struck up anew,
She sent to me the fairest flowers that grew
In sun or shade.

A sweet boquet,
Bound so unique, just as a golden sheaf,
With here and there a little silver leaf,
And verdant spray.

Applause was loud ;
And lest some freshman or some " soph," so wise,
My gesture or my speech should criticise,
I simply bowed.

When all quiesced,
Congratulations came ; and in the whirl
I had a conversation with the girl
So gaily dressed.

Beneath the stars,
And constellations then, our carriage roll'd —
We spoke of those, named by the Romans old :
" Venus and Mars."

And through the parks,
Where the silv'ry streams from the fountains play,
And dance in the moonlight, we took our way,
As gay as larks.

A senior must
On such occasions, (as they say out west
When e'er they entertain a friendly guest) ;
" Blow in his dust."

So, in her glee,
She pinned a sweet boquet upon my breast,
Which surged like the billows that cannot rest
Upon the sea.

While thus we drove,
(As seniors do,) and talked of a career,
How I'd be a president or a peer,
As time would prove ;

The hours flew by,
As you know they do with their wings so fleet,
When for the first times earnest triflers meet,
So young and shy.

It grew so late,
That lest her parents should become alarmed,
We drove along, with Cupid's arts quite charmed,
Up to her gate.

The story old,
Which has been the same for six thousand years,
With farewells and vows, with sighs and tears,
That night was told.

We met no more ;
I tramp'd the world around in search of fame,
And then back to my humble town I came,
Full sick and sore.

"She went acraft"
With a man not educat'd in the schools,
But knew well how to use a miner's tools,
And sink the shaft.

She sent their card ;
I was chagrined by my unhappy lot ;
But considered, and then determined not
To take it hard.

For such is life ;
The schools don't teach a person, now-a-days,
To work, or those most mysterious ways
To get a wife.

But t'other night,
While thinking o'er those happy hours,
And searching thro' my trunk, I found the flowers —
A lovely sight !

You could have guessed
Why I have kept them to this very day —
Not for their beauty, but the novel way
That they were pressed !

VANITY FAIR.

She is fair.   Her rubicund lips
Are bathed in smiles as I have seen
Them oft before when the muscles
Wantonly twitch, and to view
Bring her white teeth which shine as pearls.
Her features are not worn or maim'd
By cares, or mark'd by Time's rough finger.
The vital currents silently course
Beneath the surface of each cheek,
And cause a rosy hue there to linger.
Her eyes, although tame, glow like lamps,
Which shine in the chambers of her soul —
Like the gazelle's, the roe's,
Or the antelope's do they shine,
And like the fawn's eyes they are meek.
· Her hair is golden ; not disheveled
In pendant twists like the flirt's,
Or banged or frizzled or falsified ;
But like a Niobe she wears it.
Her form is like the fair Dian's,
Not stooped or bent or oddly swung,
And affected as oft you see them.
Her foot is not a Cinderella's,
But it is plain and uniform ;
Her well shapen hands are not made
Alone to touch the keys and give
A voice to the dumb piano ;
But are skilled as well in domestics.
Her words are ringing and clear cut,
As if each were a golden coin
Made in the mint of rhetoric.

She goes attired in modern dress —
Not a collection of silks, strings,
Lace, ribbon and paint with which
The belle *a mode* adorns herself ;
But as if a mind true and fixed
Had judged the fitness of the suit ;
And as she walks along the street,
Each anxions eye is turned to gaze ;
First the swell raises his eye-glass,
Nudges his pals and stares at her.
The queen of the parlors then looks
With scorn and disdain at her,
And demurely thinks — a rival.
The clerks drop their yardsticks when she
Stops athwart the charming window,
And ask of one another her name.
The business man takes off his specs,
As though he fears the glasses are
Deceiving him as through he looks.
The student, with classical eye,
Then scans her and thinks her to be
A modern Helen or a Dido.
Boot-blacks, at sight, whistle a refrain,
And even bachelors are forced
To regard her shape with a smile ;
Yet no one loves her. In the town
Scores of young men call upon her —
Call but once and never more.
Concerning her they all speak well ;
Still their actions do belie their words ;
For when they get within the walls
Of her domicile, the fountain
And springs of love evaporate,

Or freeze within the heart, as 'twere.
With her no one shares the sofa,
Or e'er enjoys a tete a tete.
All sit at a courted distance,
As if a barrier intervened.
Her single life surprises all,
And she herself begins to think
The young men curious and shy.
Now, adding not another page,
Without consulting her digestion,
I'll bring my story to a close
By telling you the direful secret,
Still, hoping that you will excuse
The unpolished proposition,
Which with these words can be expressed,
In fact not a whit too wisely,
But alas, too well : *her breath stinks!*

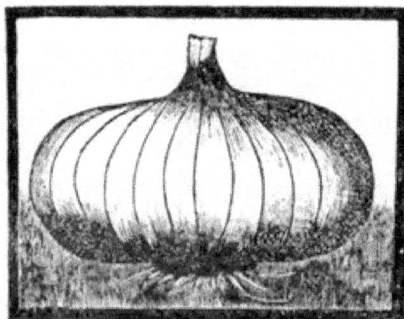

THE COMET AS SEEN WITH DIFFERENT EYES.

A PARODY.

Eyes of wonder, eyes of pleasure,
Eyes of toil and eyes of leisure,
Eyes of passion, eyes of science,
Eyes of fame and self-reliance,
Eyes of fancy, deep and dreaming,
Look to see the comet gleaming.

Men of science, with their glasses,
Are first to see it as it passes —
Think the nucl'us ne'er will crash us,
But the tail perhaps may lash us;
From them, alone, starts the rumor—
Quoth the Yankee in earnest humor;

"Waal, what's that tail made ov, Mister?
"Waal, yes, I reckon 'tis mist or——"

And the fancy, girlish dreamer;
"Has it not an awful streamer?
I wonder where it got its fashion?"

Says the swell, with smothered passion;
"Awe, her tail, though quite unhandy,
Is a reg'lar — awe Jim dandy!"

Lovers strolling, scarcely seeing
Tail or comet as 'tis fleeing —
What care they for comet gleaming,
When love's passion copes their seeming?
On his arm so fondly leaning,
Timid bride asks groom its meaning.

The soldier views it with the feeling
That war upon the land is stealing.

"Ah, what a ride !" cries the tourist ;
"But the landing's not the surest —
Yes, I know it would be splendid,
But I fear, though, never ended."

And the sailor on the ocean
Views it with a deep emotion ;
Chinaman John from his station
Best likes "tails" of his nation.

Business man of vain intention,
Would have a car of such invention,
But says the poet, "This reminds me
Of this earth on which it finds me ;
For things of life bright and glowing,
Soon are gone like comet going."

Coggia, signal of distress,
Light of etheral nothingness,
No one knows where thou art speeding
With thy huge tail thus receding.

NATURE'S SOLITUDE.

A Parody.

Afar in the country I love to ride,
With a 44 navy strapped onto my side,
Away—away from the city's dull noise,
Where the police are raising Cane with the boys,
By valleys remote where the pole-cat plays,
Where the brindle cow stoopeth adown to graze,
Where the snake and the lizard unhunted recline,
Screened by the bowers of the poisonous vine ;
Where the wild goose browses at peace in his wood,
And the mud sucker gambols unscared in the flood ;
And the wild boar whetteth his tusks at will,
And the musical mosquito drinketh his fill.

Afar in the country I love to ride,
With a 44 navy strapped onto my side,
Down through the stubble in my little bare feet,
Where the jocular bumbee hath his retreat,
In the brown sear woods to hunt the paw-paws,
Where the fierce Thomas cat sharpeneth his claws,
Mid briars and thorns where the Billy goats graze,
Alone and barefooted I LOVE to haze ;
Where the butting ram and kicking jackass,
Both starve to death for the same blade of grass,
And the red snooted buzzard wheels high o'er head,
Greedy to sniff and to gorge on the dead.

Afar in the conntry I love to ride,
With a 44 navy strapped onto my side ;
Where the smiling bulldog sits down at the gate,
With his head full of teeth and his heart full of hate,

Where the big country girl considers your ways,
And laughs at your clothes as she standeth to gaze,
Where she grins at your collar and tall plug hat,
And talks to her mother about your cravat,.
Then see her big brother with hay-seeded hair,
With his pants in his boots make ready to swear
And fume in your presence for cutting a dash,
And scold his fat sister for " making a mash."

Afar in the country I love to ride,
With a 44 navy strapped onto my side,
Where the Spanish needle cometh through to my hide,
And beggar lice into my hair become tied,
Where the boys all meet by the light of the moon,
And dive in the woods in search of the "coon,"
And steal all the chickens that roost on the fence,
And have a rare feast at their neighbor's expense,
Where they all leave me to wonder and grin,
A-holding the bag to catch the coons in,
Where I stay two days without any food,
To me, is Nature's Solitude.

THE MYSTERY OF A MUSTACHE.

This is a tale of sad mishaps,
    When virgins walked the streets,
When school-boys and the other chaps
    Were baffled by dead heats ;
Yes, then I woo'd a lass most fair,
With rosy cheeks and curly hair,
With winning ways, as light as air,
And eyes, so shy, without a stare.

Well, I was struck with that sweet face,
    How foolish one can be !
My confidence was out of place,
    Which I could never see ;
Although a lad from other climes,
Yet I was rather "green" those times —
I went to school and wrote odd rhymes,
And spent, for chewing gum, my dimes.

A harness-maker came to town.
    He was a tramp they say,
He cut my rising spirits down
    And won my girl away.
He had a cane, a faded coat,
And whiskers like a William goat,
And so, my dear began to dote,
And sent to me a saucy note.

He often with the others met
    My sweetheart in the choir,
And somehow his appearance set
    Her bosom all on fire ;
So he was introduced one night,
Which knocked me higher than a kite —
He fell in love with her at sight,
And she responded with her might.

There was no hair upon my lip,
    Of course he had me *down*,
So, when she let this secret slip,
    I never ceased to frown ;
For any mustache was to her
" A sweet incense, a spice, a myrrh,
    To tone a kiss which might occur. "

THE CAMEL'S HUMP.

'Twas during the war, eighteen sixty five —
My hero still in the states may survive —
His name ?   William Merryweather, a free,
Go-easy mortal as ever could be ;
First in the battle, and first to break ranks,
First on the camp-ground playing his pranks.

The chaplain oft lectured William on " soul ; "
But still he would drown his griefs in the bowl,
And slyly wince at the chaplain's remark,
And cling to his sins though varied and dark ;
And seemed to appear, as his name implies,
Quite Merryweather, yet cloudy his skies.

One day, while sitting outside of his tent,
And trying some trick or joke to invent,
The chaplain came up with serious frown,
And was saluted by William, the clown ;
" Say, chaplain, seein' yer always so kind,
One question answer and settle my mind."

The chaplain, anxious to see him repent,
And thinking a sin he wished to lament,
Said : " Certainly, William, I shall take pride
To answer questions you wish to confide."
" Well," William said, " since yer don't mind my slack,
Why has the camel a hump on his back ? "

" Why, William ! you and all men ought to know
That it's because God created him so!"
" No, chaplain," said William with a dry cough,
" That's jest where I think you preachers are off ;
Now, let me give you a sensible view,
And then I'll leave the whole matter with you."

" Yer see, the camel's a kind of a beast
That on briers and thistles likes to feast,
And while old Noah was buildin' the Ark,
The camel was out on his usual lark ;
When Noah had done, and blew his last note,
The camel *humped himself* to catch the boat."

EATON.

Tune — " Yankee Doodle."

Was riding in a dining car,
And eating as I traveled,
We came upon a little town,
With streets well paved and graveled :
I thought I'd ask its humble name,
Before I took my meat on ;
The carman smiled and looked at me,
And gently whispered ; " Eat on. "

O yes, I will, and plenty too,
But don't be such a flunky,
Why, if it were not for the ears,
I'd think you were a donkey!"
Why do you wish to tease a man
With your outrageous bleatin' ?
Come, tell its name, and we'll be friends —
The fiend once more yelled; " Eat on!"

Yes, of course, you see I will,
Come, won't you have a bite, sir ?
I've traveled some to see the world,
And never like to fight, sir ;
And look ! the train will soon be gone,
The engine has its heat on,
O speak the name before we go !
Once more he bellowed, " Eat on."

He waived his hand, the train sped on,
And I was left a-thinking,
That this wise man who snub'd me so,
Must surely have been drinking,
And so I asked the friendly guest,
(Who had done the treatin',)
What this omnous town was named,
He merely faltered ; " Eat on."

Eat on! Ye gods, invoke me not ;
My cup no longer sweeten,
For I have reached the maximum,
Within the town of Eaton ;
O, I have tramped about the states,
Strange lands I've had my feet on,
Ne'er have I seen a town like this,
This little town of Eat on."

.

NOT FOR ME.

I passed by her window,
    I saw the tranquil smile
Which played with her features,
    And kiss'd her lips the while.
I heard the joyous laugh,
    The merry music sound,
Then fair guests ceased to quaff,
    And dancing feet went round;
But not for me, for me.

And thro' the bright mid-night,
　And all the " wee sma' hours,"
Angels in the moonlight
　Told me: " Up to the door
They came and then away
　They drove with coach and four,
Until the break of day;
　But not for thee, for thee.

Then sought she her pillow,
　And dreamed a happy dream
Of the weeping willow,
　And the mountain stream,
Where Agustus met her;
　And as she smiled, amain,
At his wit, some fetter,
　Unseen, rack'd her with pain;
But not for thee, for thee."

I pass'd by her window,
　As oft I had before;
But the doctor's carriage
　Stood just before the door —
'Twas fever, they told me,
　And bade me take warning;
I did; but behold ye!
　A hearse called this morning;
But not for me, for me.

THE MELONCHOLERA DAYS.

A PARODY.

The meloncholera days are come,
  The saddest of the year,
The urchin leaves his chewing gum,
  The Dutchman leaves his beer.
Heaped in every grocery store
  Are melons so immense,
That any red or yellow core,
  Will only cost ten cents!

Where are the rich and tender "greens"
  That used to taste so good?
All "gorn" save the butter-beans
  Which serve us still for food.
Berries black and berries sweet
  Have now all passed away,
And yet from wagons in the street,
  I hear a cry all day.

The streets are full of rinds and seed,
  The gutters heaping lie,
The swine are choked to death in greed,
  "How is that for high?"
The "nutmeg" and the "cantelope"
Have overrun the land,
The cucumber, an early hope,
  Is still in good demand.

The boys work now, by rule compact,
    They have a *heap* of fun,
They've got so now they can *subtract*,
    Borrow and *carry* one!
But he who steals and runs away —
    So once the poet said —
Will live to steal another day,
    When melon vines are dead.

And oh, what pains do follow on
    To make him double o'er,
And wish the tempters were all gone,
    To tempt him nevermore;
For all the world should be at *piece*,
    And all should happy be,
Save him who don't know when to cease
    Should have the die-or-rhea.

THE NEW TRY AGAIN.

Should you wish to learn to smoke,
        Try, try again,
You will find it quite a joke,
        Try, try again;
It may make you spue at first,
'Till you think your skin will burst —
Take some lager for your thirst —
        Try, try again.

If you buy a " 2 for 5,"
   Try, try again,
You will have to tug and strive,
   Try, try again;

If it does not make you spue;
Then you can begin to chew;
Slyly thus combine the two,
   Try, try again.

If your breath begins to stink,
   Try, try again.
You can help it with a drink,
   Try, try again;

Then your whisky should appear,
For if you will persevere,
You can take it with your beer,
   Try, try again.

If you fancy Limberg cheese,
   Try, try again,
You can eat it when you please,
   Try, try again;

It will make your breath so sweet,
That every one you chance to meet,
Will turn from you with nimble feet,
   Try, try again.

With bad whisky and cigars,
   Try, try again,
You can smoke just like the cars,
   Try, try again;
In a contest you'd be free
To tackle any living three,
Or Vesuvius o'er the sea,
   Try, try again !

A GIRL'S SOLILOQUY ON "BANGS."

" Plague take my bangs, my hateful bangs !
 While this one curls the next one hangs!
  I've worried an hour
  With patience and power,
  Until my face itself is sour.

Committing, no doubt, fifty sins,
While twisting the unruly pins,
  And irons hot as fire;
  Next using a quire
  Of paper—to increase my ire.

I had seen in a book, somewhere,
That *gum* was good to bang the hair;
  So, then I took gum
  To make it succumb,
  Assisted, kindly, by a chum.

But I shall ne'er do that again,
For they looked like a bison's mane,
    And to my surprise
    Hung down o'er my eyes,
Not showing me a whit too wise.

Sometimes I *hate* the *name* of bangs !
Indeed, they fill my soul with pangs;
    But, being in style,
    I must, for awhile,
My wounded spirit reconcile.

However, these are of no use;
Tins, pins, gum, irons, paste and juice—
    'Tis safer to wear
    Some other girl's hair,
Who left her bangs to go "Over there."

POOR OLD POMP.

A SONG.

My poor heart's broke—
'Tis not a joke;
But I'll tell you all my grief,
    'Tis about the end
    Of a canine friend,
So, then, of course, quite brief.

Chorus—" He must have been a good dog—
  Solo—Oh, he *was* a good dog,
  And fond of play and romp.
Chorus—He must have been a big dog"—
  Solo—Oh, he *was* a big dog ;
  His given name was Pomp.

The children cried—
Chorus—"The neighbors sighed?"
But I think 'twas all pretense;
For whene'er he got
Over in their lot,
They "fired" him over the fence.

Chorus—"He fought the cats?"
But kill'd the rats—
Chorus—And chased the sheep o' nights?"
O, no, no indeed;
For his daily feed
Was loads of liver and lights.

He got a pill—
Chorus—"Which made him ill?"
'Twas a dose of pounded glass;
Yes it made him pale—
Chorus—"And curled his tail?"—
And it caused his death, alas!

I wouldn't have cried,
Because he died;
But one thought, still gives me pain;
As I stopped up street
For some sausage meat,
I found his *collar and chain!*

EXPRESSIONS OF THE UP-TOWN PEOPLE ON THESE HOT DAYS.—(A July Idyl.)

Smith—"Oh, for a pillar of Arctic snow,
　　　A coverlet made of ice,
　　　A bed where the welcome blizzards blow,
　　　Though tossing us up like dice !"

Jones—" Oh, for a ride on a glacier's side,
　　　Where shines the Aurorian light,
　　　Where hungry insects ne'er reside,
　　　Or hang around for a bite !"

Brown—" Oh, for a Borean storm surprise,
　　　Or a frozen-wind cyclone,
　　　Or for a fan of enormous size,
　　　To reach to the Frigid Zone !"

Tompkins—" Oh, for a trip on a comet's tail
　　　Through infinite depths of space,
　　　To some high peak where a cooler gale
　　　Would come to our parching face !"

Hadley--" Oh, for a sleep in an iceberg's core,
　　　In an undiscover'd bed,
　　　Where goeth not up the fretful snore
　　　From the sol'taire nose in red !"

All—But, we *get* only the scorching beam,
　　　A shifting phantom of shade,
　　　Perchance a plate of the so-called cream,
　　　Two straws and a lemonade.

Then, tell us that earth's a paradise,
    And pleasures wondrously cheap,
When we hire a boy to brush the flies,
    Whenever we wish to sleep!

THE CANDIDATE

BEFORE THE ELECTION.

" Why, how do you do, *Mister* Brown?
I'm real glad you came to town,
That I may grasp that honest hand;
We mortals are too apt to stand
On trifling ceremonies, and
Forget the welfare of the land—
How are your babies and your wife?
Those precious jewels of a life!
Well?   Good!   Come have a cigar?
No?   Well, then a smile at the bar?
Wife scolds?   Well, I always did think
We should close those places of drink!

If I'm elected, neighbor Brown,
I'll do my best to put them down—
Ah, gone ? May fortune strew your way ;
But don't *forget* your *friend*, Good day !"

AFTER THE ELECTION.

" Here comes *old* Brown, one of the cranks,
To bore me with his Nash'naĺ Banks,
The Chinese Act, Tariff and Trade,
(I wish such men were never made.)
Or with some lie of wife or brats,
(Enough to shame good Democrats.)
Or some ill-wrought petition which,
If carried 'll make the old rogue rich.
I see the blossom on his nose
Is getting redder as it grows—
I'll *have* to greet him.—Hello, Brown !
What in the world brings *you* to town ?
How can you leave your wife and kids !
(A politician never rids
Himself of old bores.   Heaven knows
I can't breathe right until he goes.)
They're well— What ! a petition, too ?
I'm sorry I can't sign it, Brown—Adieu !"

THE MODERN PRINCE.

TUNE—*A Tinker and a Tailor.*

O, he comes o'er the Atlantic
With an air that is pedantic;
And the ladies all grow frantic
    About his royal blood;
With a smile, robust and healthy,
And with words and ways so stealthy,
He tells no one he's wealthy,
    But has it understood.

He goes with the ladies yachting—
To the parks to see the trotting;
But all the while he's plotting
    Like a shrewd financier ;
Although quite aristocratic,
I am sure he is fanatic
About singers operatic,
    And gardens full of beer.

Then at the evening party,
He has a laugh so hearty.
With "gush" enough to start a
    New, turbine water wheel.
So, he tries to play casino ;
But good gracious ! What does he know ?
" How to eat a Philipino
    Made of an orange peel!"

But with ways so very airy
Does the dances like a fairy,
And they wonder who he'll marry
    Before his money's spent;
Well, he weds a banker's daughter,
'Tis a lesson sad he's taught her;
For the news comes o'er the water;
    "A fraud, without a cent!"

BRIM-FULL.

There is a hateful hat,
  Sometimes 'tis called a "flat,"
And I can't tell you whether
'Tis made of straw or feather;
  But this I'm sad to know;
  It comes where'er I go.

On Sunday in my pew,
  I thought I had a view
To see and hear the preacher;
But came therein a creature
  Who down before me sat
  With her Gainsboro hat.

I went again — to hear
  The younger Booth in "Lear." —
But ere they rang the curtain,
They ushered in a certain
  Young lady with a brim
  That made the footlights dim.

I thought I'd try a show,
  Where big hats *never* go;
But there before the cages,
Both looking wise as sages,
  Admiring monkey-whims
  Two ladies stood with brims.

So that's the way it goes
  At church, at plays, at shows;
While hiding ladies' faces
With feathers, straw, and laces,
  The broadbrims seem to take
  " The everlasting cake."

MIKE'S LITTLE DOG PRINCE.

(*Canis Finigansis.*)

I'll tell you a story of Prince,
A dog that has "lots o' good sints;"
    But plays the " Old Harry "
    With Ella and Mary,
And keeps their beaux off of the fence.

For, always, he barks in advance,
Then bites when he gets a good chance;
    For such is his failing,
    To creep through the paling,
And seize a young man by the pants.

The other girls think him "immense,"
And laugh at the numerous rents,
 And say he does right
 To bark and to bite,
And keep the boys off of the fence.

He's a terrible dog for rats,
And fights with the John Thomas cats,
 And follows "McCarty"
 From party to party,
Which bores the poor Democrats.

The loafers have learned a wise trick,
And shun the approach of the "Mick;"
 For when they see Prince,
 They flee with a wince,
And know he is nigh with his stick.

But *why* Prince's a dog of such sense,
And 's kept regardless of expense,
 Is; in days o' disaster
 He stuck to his master,
And *kept him off of the fence.*

A CAPUT-AL JOKE.

To you, perhaps, this story's old,
But once a clown, so I've been told,
O'ertook his friend upon the way,
Who thus to him began to say:
"Good morning, friend, give us a shake;
Oft'times we've met, lest I mistake;
And when I meet you as I go,
Your head is always bending low,
I ask you this, now tell me true,
Have sad misfortunes come to you,
Or are you brooding o'er the stings
That fortune to another brings?
Why not cheer up, with head on high,
And bear reverses, as do I?
"Good sir," the clown politely said,
"I've learnt some facts about the head;
I've been in fields with birds and bees,
I've been in orchards with the trees,
I've been in gardens with the fruit;
I'm satisfied beyond dispute;
I have examined heads of wheat,
And here to you let me repeat,
That *empty* heads do stand quite straight,
But *laden* heads bend down, sedate.
No man, by this, would I condemn;
But green fruit seldom bends its stem;
Since this is true of fruit and grain,
Must it not be of men and brain?"

DOG DAYS DOGGEREL.

Rays in coming down *ab solis*
  Reprove us with a searching scowl,
Till, at length, they oft patrol us
  Where mad and thirsty canines howl.

In our book we merely noted
  The points one gave us in his song ;
How he'd been a *dog*, devoted,
  And for his pains received a thong.

Saying : "I have heard my mother
  Remark : ' Each dog will have his day;'
But for me, somehow or other,
  In this shed I'm doom'd to stay.

Master said : ' His star is Sirius,
  And while it shines we'll keep him close' —
'Tis *serious*, yes, delirious,
  And also, very lachrymose !

Truly, on this point I'm puzzled;
  A dog went crazy, just next door,
And the woman had *me* muzzled
  And tethered here, hurt to the core.

Now the air is full of vapor,
    And ev'ry pond is turning green,
Master, just to cut a caper,
    Has gone where no dog can be seen.

Yet, in liquid coolness rolling,
    My master, at the ocean's side,
Bathing, driving, or a-strolling,
    Hears not the moaning of the *tied*.

THE CLASSICAL FISHERMAN.

Sometimes I take my Cicero
    To cast a Cataline,
And as upon the bay we go,
    I bait her hook and mine.

A Plat o' cat is just the thing,
    A student's mind to please—
We'd Livy life of modern king
    On fishes such as these.

Suppose we see a water-snake ?
    It won't ab Horace much—
A Juvenal of course would quake,
    And faint at sight of such.

Iphigenie footing sure'
    I climb a rugged cliff,
Until my lady's looks, demure,
    Recall me to the skiff.

And then I'll Cæsar by the hand,
    And reascend the ledge—
While on the very Virgil stand,
    She won't approach the edge.

So fishing thus along the bay,
    A summer's day we spend,
I can not Tell you in this lay,
    What happy thoughts attend.

And when the sun is sinking low,
    My lady has her wish,
For having now a prize to show,
    Takes Homer string of fish.

"NO FRUIT."

Enough, enough ye men of lore!
  Your wisdom (?) we salute;
But can't exactly have you bore
  Our lives out with " No Fruit !"

Ye tell the havoc of the frost
  That kills each tender shoot;
And how the "luckless farmer" lost
  A year's supply of fruit!

O, sapient souls! O, please desist;
  For just one day, be mute,
Don't let your truthful tongues insist
  Forever, " There's no fruit."

A tender corn we can endure,
   Perhaps, a pinching boot,
But hang the doctor who would cure
   The prophet of " the fruit ! "

We could forgive a stubborn mule,
   A " dead-beat" or "galoot;"
But heaven save us from the fool,
   Who always cries, " No fruit!"

Chain-gangs would suffer dire disgrace
   From any such recruit,
As he who goes from place to place
   With comments on " the fruit."

We'll bear the man who peddles swill,
   The chimney-sweep, in soot;
But Jove, invent a bolt to kill
   The prophet on " the fruit."

MONKEY-FACES.

Darwin says; " We sprang from the monkey."
   Now, that's rather spunky
     For a flunky—
      Monkey!

He need not try to span such a chasm
   By means of a protoplasm,
     Or any " asm;"
      Chasm!

For we think he takes the wrong basis
    To make monkey-faces
        At our races:
           Basis!

As if God had not power, all-seeing,
    To make th' human being,
        While decreeing:
           Being!

And 'tis needless for me to mention
    His book on " Descention,"
        'Tis invention.
           Mention!

People read and think about it;
    But are apt to doubt it,
        Sneer or flout it,
           Doubt it!

If he had said they came from Adam,
    Or eve, worthy madame,
        He'd 'a' had 'em.
           Adam!

A KISS.

Tune:—"Building Castles in the Air."

We live upon the sea of life,
　We're wafted by its tide;
To some there comes no day of strife,
　No friends but *bona fide*.

Sometimes I think I would enjoy
　No world as well as this;
Could I forever be the boy
　To share a maiden's kiss.

The first sweet kiss I ever stole,
　I stole from Mary Gough;
The thoughts of it still haunt my soul—
　I caught the whooping-cough !

And then, again, I recognize
　A stroll with Annie Dumps;
And how I took her by surprise,
　And took also — the mumps.

And when Kate stoop'd to whisper low,
　I kissed her like a flash;
But saints above !　I did not know
　I'd caught the scarlet rash !

And can I e'er forget sweet Nell
    Until my day of death?
For still methinks that I can smell
    The onions on her breath.

And still life's dream's a handsome face,
    Its smile a poet's bliss;
And men grow frantic in the race
    To win therefrom a kiss.

TO THE BROOM BRIGADE.*

See the "soldiers" fall in line,
Which, of course, is crinoline,
Looking sweet and half divine,
    As they march in pantomime.

See them as they quickly glide
O'er the stage from side to side,
While the gazers say with pride,
    " How they keep the step in time !"

Cap of scarlet on each head,
At each side a dust-pan red,
Brooms for muskets used instead,
    And like "reg'lars" they behave.

---

* The above was written on seeing a drill exercise at a church fair. The company consisted of the most beautiful and refined young ladies in the city. Instead of muskets they used the old fashioned brooms. The piece is written in imitation of the tune played by the orchestra, to which they drilled.

Brooms to shoulders tightly press'd,
Woman's weapon, noblest, best;
Handled nimbly and caress'd--
  O, to be a broom I crave!

Ah, fair soldier of the broom,
Thou canst sweep away my gloom—
I surrender, read my doom—
  Prisoner I, and captive slave!

IN NOVEMBER.

Now goeth forth the sportingman
  With gun upon his arm,
And blooded dog near by his side,
  Without a thought of harm.

So goeth forth the brindle cow,
  To pasture on the farm,
A-thinking of the grasses sweet,
  When summer days were warm.

The farmer "drives his team a-field,"
  To husk the ripened rows,
Before old winter comes along,
  And hides them with his snows.

"Bang, bang!" the sportsman's gun is heard,
 He thinks he saw a quail,
But oh! the brindle cow goes mad,
 And curls her festive tail.

The farmer's team then runs away,
 And he begins to yell,
And hunt the man whose gun stirr'd up
 Such everlasting —— Hades.

And then the sporting man breaks loose,
 And runs at least a mile,
Forgetting both his dog and gun,
 Which makes the farmer smile.

Then meditates the sporting man,
 That maybe he is sold,
For when he gets his dog and gun,
 The day is very cold.

A STORY OF THE BLUEBIRD !

FOR WEAK-MINDED PERSONS.

The little bluebird
In the land is heard ;
Up in the apple-tree,
'Tis singing for you and me.

Along comes a boy,
Who makes it a toy;
He picks up a stone and throws,—
Away the bluebird goes !

There again it sits,
And chirrups and twits,
Then shakes its little wings,
And triumphantly sings.

Boy thinks on a plan
Of conquest ; and can
Not keep it on his breast
Till bluebird makes its nest.

For up in the tree
He happens to see
Holes in a limb, where he
Thinks the nest ought to be.

So up, up, he goes,
Propp'd by his big toes,
And holding with his legs,
He reaches for the eggs.

Out springs a black-snake !
Boy forgets to take
Time enough to descend,
So, breaks his neck, THE END.

OVERCOATS IN JUNE.

Overcoats in June !
Why, I'd just as soon
Be compelled to emigrate to the moon
Where there is no air,
As always to wear
Overcoats and mits on occasions so rare.

Overcoats in June
A precious boon ?
Ah, this reminds me they were pull'd too soon,
Like the tender shoot,
Our unmatured fruit
Which the boy thinks a needful attribute.

I'd like to know where
The summer, so rare
Can be recruiting or taking the air—
I've heard people say
That sometime in May
Or June, *summers*, gen'rally come to stay;

But one would suppose
From the hails and snows,
And the liberality of his nose,
That Winter and Spring,
In forming a " ring,"
Had thought summer a " contemptible thing."

HEN-PECKED PHILOSOPHY.

Xantippe was a woman of her mind,
Which's frequently the case with womankind:
She was the wife of wise, old Socrates,
Who always let her manage as she'd please;
'Twas wisest, he said, although, hardly fair;
For he remembered his eyes and his hair.

Alcibiades, speaking of his wife,
Ask'd Socrates how he lived in such strife;
Explaining, that he would as soon be dead,
As to give up all the hair on his head.
" O, I expect her to abuse me thus,
And should feel lonesome not to hear her fuss,
It is as common, now, and as discreet,
As rattle of carriages in the street ! "

One day, while her anger had sway in her breast,
She used all the " names" her wrath could suggest :
In order to shun the "racket and roar,"
Wise Socrates went to sit in the door;
And, his demeanor, so quiet and tame,
Rekindled, once more, her anger to flame;
So, up the stair-steps, in a trice she fled,
And poured a pail of water on his head.
" Ah," said he laughing, " it is very plain,
That after so much thunder there'd be rain. "

THE SPRING POET.

The first poet of Spring
Attempted to sing,
But ere he could read his first verse,
The editor wise
Black'd both of his eyes,
And ordered a coffin and hearse.

The foreman with " planer"
Dealt him a brainer,
And " pied " his whole " form" on the floor,
The " devil " in gloom,
Swept up with the broom,
And carried him out at the door.

All broke up by the knocks,
He reached the " hell-box,"
Where it was the " impression" he'd stay ;
But think of the jest !
Before the inquest,
A " stiff-hunter" stole him away.

Then the " local man " wrote,
And set it to note,
The song the gay printers did sing,
That if tired of life,
Or a scolding wife ;
Just bring in a verse about " Spring."

THE STREET WALKER.

Oh, merciful stars! there she goes,
· Led by her notion and her nose—
Tramp, tramp—from morn till night she's seen,
Like a castle-guarder for the queen;
Bold and audacious, rude and rash,
On the alert, " making a mash. "

No school, no book, no magazine;
Just tramp, tramp, tramp like a marine
On the deck.   And, anon her eye
Sees new victims which need not try
To show the unmerciful lash
Of her tongue, while "making a mash. "

Counting the bricks which pave the streets,
Smiling at ev'ry " snob" she meets ;
Like the moth which flies to the blaze
In twilight of the summer days,
And for the glow loses his life,
So she, for show, becomes a wife.

O, giddy girl, O, deluded girl,
Whose head is always in a whirl,
We humbly ask you to desist,
No longer in the ranks enlist
Of those who walk and stalk the streets
To " mash" the rough and toughest " beats. "

SANDWICHES.

"Answer a fool according to his folly."—*Solomon.*

Ingersoll.—"How in the desert, I pray you tell,
Did e'er the children of Isra'l dwell,
On such a limited bill of fare?"

Orthodox.—"Why, on the manna sandwiches there."

Ingersoll.—"Let me ask you to explain, once more,
Where they obtained such bounteous store?"

Orthodox.—"Why, Ham was there, and, so it is said,
All his descendants mustered and bred."

Ingersoll.—"Stop there a moment; 'tis eas'ly seen
They had no butter to spread between;
Sandwiches arn't sandwiches, you know,
Without good butter to make them so!"

Orthodox.—"Ah, remember, when God in his ire,
Rained upon Sodom brimstone and fire.,
He told his saints to hasten and flee,
And turn not back his vengeance to see;
But, alas! Lot's wife having a fault,
Turn'd to look back — and turn'd to salt:
So, in the desert, with good intent,
All of Lot's family, but 'er went."

ON THE BANANA PEEL.

O, banana peel! O, banana peel!
Thou slippeth and slideth the trav'ler's heel;
Thou scooteth him up and letteth him drop;
Thus making of him a regular mop!

O, banana peel! O, banana peel!
Thou maketh the stoniest heart to feel;
For tossing his feet up into the air,
Thy victim is forced to utter a prayer!

O, banana peel! O banana peel!
Thou art ever a source of anger and weal,
For always playing thy slippery tricks,
A-knocking men down, yet striking no licks!

O, banana peel! O, banana peel!
Respecting no man, either rude or genteel;
But bringing down both rheumatics and gout,
And bouncing their pockets, both inside out!

THE GO-BY.*

O, I'm a millionaire,
I'll tell you what I know by,
My sweetheart made her will,
And gave to me the go-by.

*Note.—" Go-by," or " G. B." is a slang expression in the Western states meaning the grand bounce, the cold shoulder, the mitten, the sack, a square deal, a send off, a kick a blowing up, or some other word of Latin (?) origin, used, generally, by a young lady, to show her utter disgust for the unmitigating ass who endeavors to gain, by infinietismal increments, the undivided unit of her love.

O, I'll be fixed for sure,
So far across the Oby,
For down in A-si-a,
There is the desert Gobi.

A *deserted* youth I am,
Her cot my tears shall flow by,
Not for the waste of land,
But for the dreadful go-by.

ENOUGH TO DRIVE POOR OSCAR WILD.

Sunflower bonnets and sunflower hats,
Sunflower ribbons, ties and cravats,
"Sunflow'r parties," so they've been styled,
Enough to drive poor Oscar wild.

Sunflower gardens perfume the air,
Sunflower pictures everywhere,
Sunflower cards in our baskets piled —
Enough to drive poor Oscar wild.

Sunflower men make their sunflower calls,
Sunflower clubs give their sunflower balls,
Sunflower maidens, "too too" beguiled —
Enough to drive poor Oscar wild.

Yellow and black or lily white,
Is all I see from morn till night ;
Sunflower dresses for ev'ry child—
Enough to drive poor Oscar wild.

Sunflower gossip is all I hear,
Sunflowers bloom twelve months in the year :
O, sunflower man, so soon exiled —
Enough to drive poor Oscar Wilde.

PLAYING BUTTON.

Tune—"Gypsy Davy."

O, "button" is a merry game,
  And glad am I to play it ;
But children aren't the only ones
  Who ever learn to play it.

The little lambs, they skip and jump
  To exercise their mutton,
And then they play that little game,
  The little game of buttin' !

But when they break their little necks
  With their caper cutting,
They never have to stop and ask;
  " Who has got the butting ?"

When Carlo finds a bite of meat,
  He eats it like a glutton—
Forgets about the other dogs,
  Because he has the button.

Some nosy eds. won't clip this piece,
  While other squibs they're cuttin',
But turn their inky snoots aloft,
  And say : " 'S not worth a button."

TWO,

Two souls with but a single thought,
  Two hearts that bill and coo;
He said, " I am oor sugar plum,
  Oose sugar, sugar plum are oo ?"

She smiled a sweet, molasses smile,
  And blushed as red as morn,
And threw her arms about his neck,
  And gently whispered, "Oorn."

Two shadows, then, upon the wall,
  Were melted into one,
Then two eyes with their lustrous light,
  Were glowing like the sun !

*   *   *   *   *

The eastern sky was turning gray,
  A wakeful cock, then crew;
Two lovers parted in the hall,
  The old house-clock struck "two,"

TO HATTIE.

" Flattery makes the wise feel flatter."
　　But then, you've experienced that,
Then, should I be blamed in the matter
　　Of simply admiring a Hat ?

In selecting, I tell my hatter,
　　" Give me a hat that will wear,
And keep its right shape and not tatter,
　　Or fade in changes of air."

And just so with the friends who scatter
　　Smiles from their faces so fair,
I care not so much for the latter,
　　Unless they're friends who will wear.

TO SMITH ON HIS MARRIAGE.

O, man of that *peculiar* name,
　　Regarded as a myth,
How could you ask a blushing dame
　　To call herself " Mrs. Smith ?"

MARRIED IN HASTE.

BEFORE THE ORANGE BLOSSOMS.

He was like the towering oak,
She like the clinging vine,
She wore a costly sealskin cloak,
He wore his diamonds fine.

AFTER THE BLOSSOMS.

Alas, alas for towering oak,
Alas, for clinging vine,
They have their jewels in the "soak,"
And live on tenderline.

THE BUTTER FLY.

What doth make the butter fly?
Buckwheat cakes, and chicken pie,
Oyster soup and oyster fry,
    Or the miller.

Yes, and something else, my dear,
Listen now and you shall hear,
It is ugly, but don't fear —
    The caterpillar.

THE LAST.

O, what was that the cobbler flung
　　To hit his wife, while he aghast,
Received the missiles from her tongue,
　　Which always craved the *very last?*

O, what is first to wear our shoes,
　　To give them shape and hold them fast,
And make us have the bluest blues,
　　Because too small?　Why, 'tis the last!

And what is it that's number 8,
　　With no excuse for being vast?
To say the word I hesitate;
　　But now 'tis said — it is my last!

CONTENTS.

www.ingramcontent.com/pod-product-compliance
Lightning Source LLC
Chambersburg PA
CBHW030619270326
41927CB00007B/1235